THE UNITED STATES
AND THE WORLD:
SETTING LIMITS

The Francis Boyer Lectures on Public Policy

THE UNITED STATES
AND THE WORLD:
SETTING LIMITS

Jeane J. Kirkpatrick

American Enterprise Institute for Public Policy Research

ISBN 0-8447-1379-1

Library of Congress Catalog Card Number 86-70364

Printed in the United States of America

American Enterprise Institute
1150 Seventeenth Street, N.W., Washington, D.C. 20036

The
Francis Boyer Lectures
on Public Policy

The American Enterprise Institute has initiated the Francis Boyer Lectures on Public Policy to examine the relationship between business and government and to develop contexts for their creative interaction. These lectures have been made possible by an endowment from the SmithKline Beckman Corporation in memory of Mr. Boyer, the late chairman of the board of the corporation.

The lecture is given by an eminent thinker who has developed notable insights on one or more aspects of the relationship between the nation's private and public sectors. Focusing clearly on the public interest, the lecture demonstrates how new conceptual insights may illuminate public policy issues and contribute significantly to the dialogue by which the public interest is served.

The man or woman delivering the lecture need not necessarily be a professional scholar, a government official, or a business leader. The lecture should concern itself with the central issues of public policy in contemporary America—pointing always in the direction of constructive solutions rather than merely delineating opposing views.

Lecturers may come from any walk of life—academia, the humanities, public service, science, finance, the

v

mass media of communications, business, and industry. The principal considerations determining the selection are the quality and appositeness of the lecturer's thought, rather than his or her formal qualifications.

The Francis Boyer Lecture is delivered annually in Washington, D.C., before an invited audience. The lecturer is selected by the American Enterprise Institute's distinguished Council of Academic Advisers, and the lectureship carries an award and stipend of $10,000. The American Enterprise Institute publishes the lecture as the Francis Boyer Lectures on Public Policy.

Francis Boyer Award Recipients

1977   *The Honorable Gerald R. Ford*
1978   *The Honorable Arthur F. Burns*
1979   *Paul Johnson*
1980   *William J. Baroody, Sr.*
1981   *The Honorable Henry A. Kissinger*
1982   *Hanna Holborn Gray*
1983   *Sir Alan Walters*
1984   *The Honorable Robert H. Bork*
1985   *The Honorable Jeane J. Kirkpatrick*

FOREWORD

The events of AEI's Public Policy Week traditionally culminate in the Francis Boyer Lecture on Public Policy. During the days preceding this, the Ninth Annual Francis Boyer Lecture, we conducted seminars and heard remarks from a number of government policy makers, business leaders, and scholars.

Our purpose was to explore some of the most important public policy problems facing the United States and the world: the possibility of a financial crisis in the United States, the unemployment rate in this country, the consequences of population loss in the West, the Middle East situation, and growing protectionism in international trade. This Boyer lecture enlarges on the theme of U.S. responsibilities in a world of clashing values.

The generous support of the SmithKline Beckman Corporation makes possible the Francis Boyer Award and Lecture. It is named for the late chairman of SmithKline whose diligent pursuit of truth and intellectual integrity are a beacon to all of us.

Each year AEI's Council of Academic Advisers chooses the Francis Boyer lecturer. Paul W. McCracken is chairman of the council; the other members are Donald Hellmann, D. Gale Johnson, Robert A. Nisbet, Herbert Stein, Murray L. Weidenbaum, and James Q. Wilson.

In her address, Ambassador Kirkpatrick speaks "as one having authority" — an authority not gained through academic endeavor alone but also in that fierce arena of competing ideas and ideologies, the United Nations. In her lecture, she urges us to align our foreign policy with the national interest, an effort that she assures us will be rewarded with a clearer concept of our role in international events and with the achievement of goals that have so far eluded us.

Like earlier Francis Boyer lectures, Ambassador Kirkpatrick's remarks reflect AEI's continuing commitment to the betterment of the public policy process and to the conviction that the competition of ideas is fundamental to a free society.

Last year's recipient of the award, Judge Robert Bork, introduced Ambassador Kirkpatrick.

Bill Baroody Jr.

WILLIAM J. BAROODY, JR.
President
American Enterprise Institute

INTRODUCTION

It is a distinct honor to introduce the Honorable Jeane Kirkpatrick, the recipient of the 1985 Francis Boyer Award.

This introduction is also distinctly awkward since AEI, which is apparently run by either the editors of *Reader's Digest* or the old German General Staff, has allotted me precisely eighty-seven seconds to summarize one of the richest careers in American academic and public life.

The academic career alone was a formidable one, placing her among the most productive and creative scholars in her field. Jeane Kirkpatrick studied, taught, and wrote about political science, producing five books and innumerable articles, and becoming, just before a wider world became aware of her, the Leavy Professor at Georgetown University and a senior fellow at the American Enterprise Institute.

Ms. Kirkpatrick accomplished this despite a very considerable handicap, what one columnist has called "her impolitic concern for intellectual clarity." Clarity is not universally admired, or practiced, in the academic world any more than it is in the world of politics. But she had one reader who found her clarity and her intellectual force just what the United States needed in formulating its positions internationally. It takes only one reader, if he turns out to be the president of the United States.

This must have presented Professor Kirkpatrick with something of a quandary—to continue the intellectual life, at which she excelled, or to step into a political world largely foreign to her.

Fortunately for us, Professor Kirkpatrick was familiar with Emerson's dictum about adult education. He said, "The best university that can be recommended to a man of ideas is the gauntlet of the mobs." So Jeane Kirkpatrick went to the United Nations as our permanent representative.

Because of her, the low, often scurrilous, politics that have come to mark that institution became, at least marginally, somewhat higher and less scurrilous. The best and freest nation in the world was represented by a powerful and incisive mind coupled to a clear, unflagging moral sense. Bashing the United States, its allies, and the values of democracy is somewhat less fun if an American representative of wit and courage is ready to answer, and answer so that it stings.

Since then we have enjoyed and profited from her clarity, her gift for phrase, in other forums as well. There was, for example, the Republican National Convention. Of course, the capacity for the memorable phrase she demonstrated on that occasion is not without its costs for the rest of us. My wife and my daughter are both avid fans of Jeane Kirkpatrick. In the morning I try to read the sports pages, but my daughter, who is reading the Op-Ed pages of a paper that shall be nameless, keeps crying out, "But then they always blame America first."

We are indebted to her for much that has clarified our public discourse, for reminding us, for example, that there are important differences between authoritarian and totalitarian regimes and that international morality, like all morality, is a question of the available alternatives. We are in her debt as well for her repeated demonstration of the fallacy of regarding the superpowers as morally equivalent.

Many of us have a suspicion, however, that our reasons for being indebted to this lady lie mostly in the future. May it be so.

She has written, "Ideas have consequences; bad ideas have bad consequences." We are now about to hear some very good ideas in her speech on the subject of "The United States and the World: Setting Limits." I give you the Honorable Jeane Kirkpatrick.

JUDGE ROBERT H. BORK
U.S. Court of Appeals,
District of Columbia Circuit

THE UNITED STATES AND THE WORLD: SETTING LIMITS

We Americans have strange problems with foreign policy. We do not know what it is for. Examples of dislocation can be found on almost any day in almost any newspaper.

Today's *Washington Post,* for example, reports that the State Department is "concerned by Congressional moves to revoke Romania's trade benefits with the United States." The story goes on to say that last year U.S. trade with Romania totaled $1.2 billion with the balance "tilted heavily in Romania's favor." It added that the trade is very important to Romania's very repressive government. The State Department seeks to continue most-favored-nation treatment for Romania in the expectation that it will encourage that country's independence from the Soviet Union.

Someone, somewhere has doubtless already described U.S. favors as reflecting a "pragmatic" approach to foreign policy. Someone, somewhere surely will describe the effort to revoke Romania's most-favored-nation status as an ideological approach to foreign policy.

But will anyone, anywhere investigate the impact of most-favored-nation status on Romania's independence during the past decade or examine the effect of most-favored-nation status on the U.S. trade deficit, even in this year of preoccupation with deficits? After all, every half billion helps. Maybe a careful study has just been made of the costs and benefits to the United States of Romania's trade status. But I doubt it.

I have no special interest tonight in Romania or in U.S.-Romanian relations, any more than I have any special interest in economic aid to Ghana, India, or Zimbabwe.

I might have chosen a hundred other examples to make the point that a great many American dollars are spent and a great many U.S. assets, tangible and intangible, are consumed without much reflection—public or private, official or unofficial—on their relative contribution to our national interests. I believe that real progress has been made during this administration in ending policies clearly damaging to the U.S. position in the world. But there remains a good deal to be done. It will be done only as we come to think more realistically about the limits of our resources and more clearly about what foreign policy is for.

Strange assumptions are made concerning our power, our vulnerability, and our purposes. Often, discussion sounds as though we were an omnipotent, invulnerable, and purely altruistic people, when we are, in fact, none of these. We are vulnerable, capable of being destroyed in minutes. Our resources are limited. We, like all other nations, need a foreign policy that gives priority to our national security.

Yet, strange reactions occur when the U.S. national interest is invoked as the basis for deciding for or against a particular foreign policy. Not infrequently, people assume that decisions made on the basis of the national interest are *selfish* decisions.

Often people react as if the national interest were value free and amoral, as if it took no account of freedom, democracy, human rights, and the civilization of which we are a part. In fact, all these good things—our freedom, our prosperity, and our civilization—depend on the strength of our country. If our strength and our wealth—our national interests—are not protected, the moral goods we value will be at risk as well.

Is there really a problem with this self-evident proposition? I believe there is, and that it is very serious.

My personal encounter with this problem began after my appointment to the United Nations. The president and I both assumed that my job would be to represent the United States in that body. How surprised I was to discover many, perhaps most, Americans interested in the United Nations assumed otherwise. They thought the job of the U.S. permanent representative was to represent the United Nations to the American people.

For such people, the U.S. national interest has disappeared almost entirely into a vague notion of a stable world order embodied by the UN, which it was presumably our function to serve. American interest was identified with altruistic, abstract, universal, unrealistic, often utopian goals. What was good for anybody, it was assumed, was good for the United States.

Naturally I began to reflect on these assumptions and to read about them. I was quickly reminded that it had not always been thus. None of the current problems emerged during our first century.

That famous traveler Alexis de Tocqueville noted then that our virtues were not relevant to foreign affairs, and his observations concerning our lack of aptitude for foreign affairs foreshadowed the principal criticisms of such twentieth century scholars as Hans Morgenthau, Walter Lippmann, George Kennan, and a host of others. These men all noted that the U.S. approach to foreign affairs lacks the major strengths of our domestic politics. We lack, they have noted, a clear, stable sense of national interest that would guide us in international politics much as self-interest guides in personal affairs. And they also emphasized that we had an exaggerated expectation that conflicts among nations could be effectively dealt with by legal and judicial means.

But none of these problems emerged during our first century. The struggle for independence and nation building inculcated in our Founding Fathers a preference for proximate, concrete interests (which Tocqueville feared would be missed in foreign affairs). George Washington, Alexander Hamilton, John Adams, Thomas Jefferson, and others manifested a clear-eyed appreciation of the national interest. Washington's famous warning emphasized precisely the sense of concrete interest that bourgeois republics have been famous for.

So did Alexander Hamilton admonish against U.S. entry into a war in support of France. He argued in *Americanus*, although we support the cause of liberty and are grateful to France, the degree of service we could render by participating in the conflict was unlikely to compensate the evils that would probably flow from it to ourselves. Yes, we Americans were grateful to France for her help to us during our own war of independence, but the rule of morality is not precisely the same between nations as between individuals. He wrote,

> The duty of making its own welfare the guide of its actions is much stronger upon the former [a nation] than on the latter [an individual]; in proportion to the greater magnitude and importance of national compared with individual happiness, to the greater permanency of the effects of national

than of individual conduct. ("Pacificus: A Defense of Neutrality," July 10, 1793)

We were born an eighteenth century, liberal nation but we emerged from the nineteenth century with the economic institutions of a developed free market system and the utilitarian assumptions that accompany it. Slowly, the sense of *national* interest seems to have been dissolved by these assumptions into *individual* interests. It reemerged as "the greatest good of the greatest number."

For a century, American foreign affairs were guided by the founding generation's distrust of U.S. involvement in European politics, its memory of the costs of participation in four wars before our war of independence, and a strong, clear sense of the U.S. national interests. The experience of European wars, the distaste for Europe's seemingly endless rivalries, and the insulation of two oceans produced nearly a century of peace. In the twentieth century this period from 1812 to 1917 came to be disdained in the United States as isolationist. But, in fact, it was a century of peace in which America prospered.

During that century of peace, in which our prosperity increased, the sense of our invulnerability and of our exceptional qualities grew, along with our idealism. The tendency to think of ourselves as having a unique mission in the world grew and along side it a tendency to believe that whatever problem existed in the world was our problem.

Woodrow Wilson embodied all these tendencies and also the conviction that we could resolve international problems as we resolved problems at home and that it was our business to do so. He thought we could resolve international problems as the Founding Fathers had resolved domestic problems—with a union based on a good constitution. And so he participated very ardently in writing the Constitution of the League of Nations.

Wilson's conviction of the unique moral mission of the United States was matched by his confidence that international conflict could be eliminated by good international agreements and by a good international organization.

The American conviction that a proper world organization could prevent conflict among nations was not disturbed by what followed. Neither the rise of murderous regimes between the two world wars nor World War II itself really shook the growing American conviction that a good constitution for a good international organization could solve our problems. As a matter of fact, the rise of these murderous regimes and World War II were interpreted not as casting doubt on the ability of an international organization to maintain peace, but as proving what a terrible mistake it had been for the United States not to join the League of Nations.

Franklin Roosevelt and his advisers seemed as confident as Wilson that a well-constructed global organization could and would ensure peace forever. Even that great realist Harry Truman had great confidence that the United Nations could and would maintain peace.

Now, if they had been right and the United Nations had been able to maintain world peace, then the United States could have no greater interest in the world than the support of that organization. From the founding of the UN, U.S. interests were perceived by many as identical with the world's interest in peace. We really believed that a global democracy would work. We really believed that all the nations in the world shared our commitment to the values of democracy and our commitment to peace. We quite simply projected American values and democratic values onto all the nations of the world, and then we wrote a constitution—the UN Charter—that embodies that projection.

This act of projecting our values onto the whole world made it possible for us to speak of a world community, which, like all communities, was glued together by shared basic values. All people and all governments were assumed to value peace more than they wanted any of the goals incompatible with peace.

We did not really doubt that in case an outlaw arose among nations and failed to value peace adequately, the other member nations of the United Nations would, through their commitment to collective security, join together to bring the outlaw nation to task and restore order in the world. Just as a posse in a frontier town rounds up a law-breaker and members of that posse risk their lives in doing so, other nations, we believed, would have a strong enough commitment to collective security that, if necessary, they would go to war to maintain peace. In other words, we assumed that a harmony of interests, which is a guiding principle for us in our economic and political domestic life, also exists in international affairs.

Now, of course, it just did not work out. There was a very serious falsification of reality present from the very beginning. From the beginning, the United Nations included countries that did not cherish democratic values and that manifestly were not ready to forgo the use of force in their own foreign policy. In the years since, it has been demonstrated that there is no "world community." There are no values shared by all peoples and all governments. There is no international global machinery for peace keeping and peace making. The United Nations cannot preserve the values not shared and supported by its member states. This conclusion is, in fact, inescapable if one examines the record. It sounds harsh. I'm sorry. So be it.

The U.S. national interest, therefore, cannot be identical with that of all nations, some of whom do not share our most fundamental principles and interests. Neither can it be identical with the United Nations itself.

The idea of a natural harmony of interest among governments cannot survive much direct contact with reality. A good many governments want something more than they want peace. The Ayatollah Khomeini wants to depose Saddam Hussein more than he wants peace, and thousands of his followers want a passport to heaven, signed by the Ayatollah Khomeini, more than they want peace. The Vietnamese want Cambodia more than they want peace. Manifestly, the Soviets want the conquest of Afghanistan more than they want peace. Muammar Qaddafi wants Chad, the Sudan, Tunisia, Egypt, and God knows what else more than he wants peace. The hijackers of the Egyptian airliner in Malta, who shot Israelis and Americans at point-blank range and after each murder ran through the aisles singing and dancing, are not easily fit into conceptions of natural harmony. Our conceptions of natural harmony simply will not accommodate the predilection for violence and a contempt for one another's right to survive.

The fact that other governments may have deeply held goals that conflict with world order and world stability still seems to us so implausible as to be virtually incredible. This is, of course, not a new idea. George Kennan was talking about it forty years ago. He put it this way:

> To the American mind, it is implausible that people should have positive aspirations, and ones that they regard as legitimate, more important to them than the peacefulness and orderliness of international life. From this standpoint, it is not apparent

why other peoples should not join us in accepting the rules of the game in international policies, just as we accept such rules in the competition of sport in order that the game not become too cruel and too destructive and may not assume an importance we did not mean it to have.

We fall back again to imagining that profound conflicts in national goals are simply misunderstandings and that if only we understood each other better the apparent conflicts would in fact be dissolved. We think that others' goals only seem incompatible with ours. But our illusions do not contribute to the achievement of our goals.

Efforts to preserve our illusion of universal harmony have twice led our nation into war, the first time in Korea and the second time in Vietnam. I do not mean to say that these wars were not noble wars and that they were not worth fighting. I do mean to say that we were led into them by the belief that aggression must not be permitted to pay. We thought that we, along with a dwindling company of nations, could serve as a kind of world policeman, like a sheriff in a frontier town bringing an outlaw to justice. We spent a great many American lives as well as a great deal of American treasure that way. My point is not that these wars were not worth fighting. My point is that the illusion of world order, and of a central U.S. role in maintaining it, led us into wars that we almost surely would never have been involved in, if we had been operating from some less expansive conception of what we were doing in the world.

I believe that our national self-conception grew progressively expansive and at the same time we grew progressively careless about our strengths. There developed a kind of negative correlation between our expectations and our ability to accomplish our goals in the world. More and more, we also lived off of illusions about our power and vulnerability. In the years following World War II, we grew accustomed to thinking of ourselves—our country—not only as stronger than anybody but very nearly as stronger than everybody. We really nearly were. And the stronger we were (we felt), the less we needed to be concerned about the economical use of our resources.

Of course, this has all changed. The rising power and productivity of the nations of Western Europe have been magnified by the development of the European Community. The rising technological and economic power of Japan has been accompanied by the impressive performance of other countries in the Pacific Basin. The Soviet Union's dramatic growth in military power has been accompanied by the growth of the empire that today extends the Soviet reach to every continent in the world except North America.

But we have not taken as much note as we might of the growing strength of other nations and our own comparative weakness. No longer are we stronger than everybody. It is not clear that we are stronger than anybody.

One of the problems, of course, of making the U.S. national interest the centerpiece of our foreign policy is debate about what that national interest is. George Kennan's approach to foreign policy, which has always had the national interest as its center, has been criticized by those who insist that it is all very well to talk about defending the national interest, but what is it, after all? There is not really any agreement about it, we are told.

I believe these difficulties are very greatly exaggerated. Almost everyone can agree that the protection of our national interest requires, at a very minimum, protecting our country against aggression, intimidation, or conquest by a foreign power. Virtually everyone can agree that the defense of the national interest also requires maintaining the domestic bases of our national defense, including, of course, domestic industries with vital strategic importance. This, in turn, requires maintaining access to raw materials of vital strategic importance.

Most would also agree that the protection of our national interest gives us an important stake in the survival of a world of independent nations and especially the survival of nations with whom we share a civilization. I don't think it is so difficult to identify what the national interest is.

Now, what would be the consequences for foreign policy of a self-conscious assumption that we had limited resources and that we faced a powerful and dangerous potential adversary in a protracted competition and that, because we have limited resources and face protracted competition with powerful adversaries, we had best husband our resources and protect our national interests? What would we do if we made that assumption?

We would reexamine a great many of our commitments, some of our arrangements for defense, and our economic policies. We would ask concerning each commitment, How does this policy contribute to the American national interest?

What would that mean, for example, to NATO? I don't think it would mean the end of NATO at all. But NATO, like most of our international arrangements, does reflect the realities of a past age. When NATO developed, we were very strong and our allies in Western Europe were very weak. We organized NATO on the principle of "from each according to his ability, to each according to his needs." NATO has been a colossal success, of course. The strength of the polities, economies, and societies of our NATO partners is itself the most eloquent tribute to the success of NATO.

Both the circumstances in which NATO was created and the arrangements for NATO's operation, however, have changed and changed quite dramatically with its success. The distribution of threat has also been altered along with the distribution of wealth. We do not talk much about the distribution of threat in NATO. Sometimes I reflect on the fact that although the NATO treaty commits its members to respond to an attack on one as though it were an attack on all, NATO was conceived at a time when Europe was considered the only likely target. Today, that has changed. Today, the United States is also at risk.

Yet discussion in Europe about war between the superpowers often leaves out Western Europe. Talk of war "over the heads of the Western Europeans" leaves me wondering from time to time about whether our European allies are prepared today to affirm that they would consider an attack on the United States tantamount to an attack on their own nations. If so, why are they so little concerned with the security of our flanks? I am not sure whether people do not think about this question, or whether it is simply too painful to raise.

I believe giving a proper, central concern to our national interest would lead us to reexamine some other commitments. It would lead us, surely, to examine defense responsibilities in the Pacific region, where Japan enjoys great strength without equivalent responsibility. It would lead us to reexamine some of our trade commitments.

A clearer conception of the U.S. national interest would transform our conception of our relations with the

Soviet Union. I believe the United States has no unique rivalry whatsoever and that the United States has no unique interest in countering Soviet expansion.

We and all of our friends and all of our adversaries ought to be clear that *in no sense is the United States involved in a contest with the Soviet Union for world dominance.* Our disagreements with the Soviet Union are no different from those with any other country that seeks to maintain its own independence and hopes for a world of independent nations.

Our differences with the Soviet Union, then, are no different from the differences of France, the United Kingdom, Brazil, Argentina, Japan, Indonesia, China, Saudi Arabia, or any other country with the Soviet Union.

The notion of superpower rivalry and the talk of East-West struggle that uniquely involves the United States and the Soviet Union confuse us about our responsibilities and confuse many other nations about who we are and what we are doing in the world today.

I think we should make it clear that all nations who seek to maintain their own independence have a primary responsibility for doing so. If this is made clear, then the stake of all nations in developing regional alliances to reinforce and protect their independence will also be clearer. By clarifying the limits of our responsibilities and resources and making clear that we will help others help themselves as is consistent with our interests and principles, we would encourage the development and reinforcement of national self-defense and of regional alliances perhaps more effectively than we do today.

Facing the limits of our resources and our interests means giving up the illusion that we can solve all the world's problems, cure all the world's ills. It means forswearing the illusion that we are strong enough or wise enough or good enough to do so. It means treating our own needs with greater respect.

In international life and foreign policy, as in private life, recognition of one's limits is a prerequisite to effective action, and self-respect is a prerequisite to respect for others and to relations based on mutual respect. By expecting less of ourselves and being clearer about it, we can accomplish a good deal more. And we can be more certain of passing on our great, but limited, resources and our freedom to our posterity.